LIVING A

GOLDEN

LIFE

© 2017

Portions previously published as *Favorable Conditions* in
2008

Dedicated to my grandmothers Julia Lenore Wilkerson-Nelson and Theresa Eleanor Chase-Brown... the women who taught me how to navigate life's challenges with dignity, class and grace.

ACKNOWLEDGEMENTS

Rev. Joanna Gabriel – my mentor, prayer partner and friend. I love you, I appreciate you and I thank God for you.

Rev. Shaheera Stevens – thank you for inspiring and encouraging me.

Patricia GorDon – thank you for graciously opening your home to me on such a regular basis.

Pamela Heard, Dr. Bessie Fletcher, David Szymborski, Monica Kelly, Milagros Pinal and Rechelle Taylor – the most awesome board of trustees any minister could ever hope to work with. Thanks to all of you, Unity Golden Life Ministries is the growing, thriving ministry that it is today.

TABLE OF CONTENTS

FOREWORD

When this book was first published in 2008, it was called *Favorable Conditions*. That initial publication was and remains a guide for anyone and everyone who has labored under the burden of false ideas and beliefs about themselves. Nearly all of these labels have been part of the psyche since childhood. The truth that we are all perfect in the eyes of God, and born in perfection has been conditioned, taught and in some cases even coerced out of our consciousness – usually by the time we are five years of age. *Favorable Conditions*, and now its new incarnation – *Living a Golden Life* – are tools that we can all use to clear away those untruths and get to the core of our true being... claiming our collective truths and seeing ourselves the way God sees us – healthy, whole and vibrant, filled with divine energy in mind, body and soul.

Since that initial publication date, I have received e-mails and telephone calls from countless people who were able to relate to the message and supporting exercises contained in *Favorable Conditions*. Many went so far as to add that they wished they had a tool like this when they were much, much younger.

As time went on, I considered how those people expressed such deep gratitude and decided to revisit *Favorable Conditions* with the intention of re-releasing it as it was originally published. *Living a Golden Life* is an expansion of *Favorable Conditions*. Much of the content remains unchanged. However, *Living a Golden Life* goes deeper and has expanded exercises at the end of each chapter. It also contains an Epilogue which is meant to be used over and over again, many years after you finish your first reading of *Living a Golden Life*.

I encourage you to not only read this book, but to read it with a journal or notebook at your side. Take notes; record your thoughts and reactions; highlight those passages that speak to you; and complete all of the exercises at the end of the chapters. Some may find *Living a Golden Life* a useful tool for certain book clubs or discussion groups as well.

Namaste'

Vernelle

INTRODUCTION

What Is Prosperity?

*pros.per.i.ty (pros-pĕr'ê-tē) n., pl. **ties**.
The condition of being prosperous and
having good fortune or financial
success.*

Even Webster has a hard time defining prosperity. Don't you just hate it when they use the root word to define the word you're looking up? So, let's look up prosperous and see what they have to say about that.

*pros.per.ous (pros-pèr-ês) adj. **1**. Having
success; flourishing.
2. Well-to-do; well off.
3. Propitious; favorable. – **prosperously**
adv. – **prosperousness** n.*

Now, let's take a closer look at the first definition of the word prosperous – *having success; flourishing*. What kind of success? Flourishing in what way? As we look at Webster's second attempt to define the word, we find *well-to-do; well-off*. Shall we assume they're talking about money and all that it can buy? What about the third definition? *Propitious* [what a lofty word – let's not waste time looking up that one]; *favorable* [to whom?]

Of all the definitions for this seemingly simple word, I tend to like the very last definition best. However, the question remains… favorable to whom?

In the opening paragraph of their book *All About Prosperity and How You Can Prosper*, Jack and Cornelia Addington say "Prosperity is a state of mind that carries over into every area of living – health, wealth, happiness and companionship." Now that's a definition I can wrap my head around. It is clear, concise and makes perfect sense.

Prosperity is NOT money. It is NOT success. It is NOT about who has the most marbles at the end of the day. Prosperity is a state of mind. It is inside of us. Therefore, with this in mind, to whom are we favorable or unfavorable? To ourselves.

Each of us is born with all we will ever need to have total and complete prosperity in every aspect of our lives. The problem is, by the time we're old enough to talk, most of us are conditioned to believe that we're incapable of achieving anything positive without the approval and sanction of others. That happened innocently enough. Parents, grandparents, other family members and friends applaud a baby's first tooth, first step and first word. As babies grow and start exploring their world through crawling and then walking, they are told "no, no" so often that many children say "no" before they say "Mama." We'll take a closer look at this later on.

The purpose of this book is to help us see that we need no one's approval. All we need to do is look to the God spirit within to have the joy, peace, love, health and wealth we are meant to have. It's not about the money. It's about our state of mind. Thousands if not millions of books have already been written on the subject. In fact, I believe I've read about a quarter of them over the last two or three decades. Why so many? Why not just one and be done with it? The answer is simple. Each and every minute of each and every day, we are bombarded with messages contradictory to our divine nature. It is up to us to counter that barrage of negativity with constant reminders that we are spiritual beings have a human experience – not human beings having a disastrous mortal experience with nothing to look forward to but the next train wreck, bridge collapse,

12

terrorist attack, tsunami, wild fire, hurricane, earthquake, tornado or avalanche.

We have been conditioned to live in fear. The Course in Miracles teaches that it is up to us to recognize these fear tactics as nothing more than attempts to control our subconscious minds and to keep us away from the true joy that is ours.

This particular book is the second edition of yet one more in that long list of books designed to help us reclaim our joy. What I've done here is pull quotes and ideas from some of my favorites, add my own insights and comments in the form of short essays and compile them in such a way as to make it easy and fun to read. At the end of each chapter is an exercise which helps bring the point home for the reader. [Don't you just hate it when you know in advance that you're going to be asked to do something on your own?]. These exercises are designed to be fun, not hard work. Depending upon your outlook, a couple may be a little uncomfortable, but nobody will know if you do them or not. I believe you'll find that even the uncomfortable exercises will turn out to be fun if and when you decide to take them on.

When this book was first published, the title was *Favorable Conditions.* I chose that title to demonstrate that we are all capable of and entitled to claiming favorable conditions in every aspect of our lives. This time around, I decided to rename the original text and call it *Living a Golden Life* because I sincerely believe that we should all live our lives as if they are golden. Back in 2004 Jill Scott recorded a song called "Golden" which has become my personal theme song. I adopted the hook as my personal mantra… "I'm livin' my life like it's golden". The lyrics are some of the most powerful I have ever heard.

I'm taking my freedom
Pulling it off the shelf
Putting it on my chain
Wear it around my neck
I'm taking my freedom
Putting it in my car
Wherever I choose to go
It will take me far

I'm livin' my life like it's golden
Livin' my life like it's golden
Livin' my life like it's golden, golden
Livin' my life like it's golden
Livin' my life like it's golden, golden

I'm taking my own freedom
Putting it in my song
Singing loud and strong
Grooving all day long
I'm taking my freedom
Putting it in my stroll
I'll be high-steppin' y'all
Letting the joy unfold

I'm livin' my life like it's golden
Livin' my life like it's golden
Livin' my life like it's golden, golden
Livin' my life like it's golden
Livin' my life like it's golden, golden

I'm holding on to my freedom
Can't take it from me
I was born into it
It comes naturally
I'm strumming my own freedom
Playing the god in me

Representing his glory
Hope he's proud of me

I'm livin' my life like it's golden
Livin' my life like it's golden
Livin' my life like it's golden, golden
Livin' my life like it's golden
Livin' my life like it's golden, golden

I'm living my life like its golden

I'm livin' my life like it's golden
Livin' my life like it's golden
Livin' my life like it's golden, golden
Livin' my life like it's golden
Livin' my life like it's golden, golden

Livin' my life like it's golden
It really matters to me, oh
I'm living my life like its golden

Written by Matt Nolen, Tommy Lee James, Emily Marie Shackelton • Copyright © Universal Music Publishing Group, BMG Rights Management US, LLC

I sincerely hope you enjoy reading *Living a Golden Life* as much as I enjoy sharing it.

SECTION ONE

I JUST WANT A PROSPEROUS LIFE.

HOW CAN I ACCOMPLISH THAT?

CHAPTER 1

The Best Place to Start Is at The Beginning

Being prosperous is not something that we become. We already *are* prosperous. Reclaiming our God-given gifts of joy, health, peace of mind and all that prosperity means to us is not difficult – though not all that easy either if we are bound to traditional conditioning. It is up to us to release ourselves from that conditioning and change our minds about who and what we are in order to achieve true prosperity in every aspect of our lives.

In the 1960s, Bill Cosby released a comedy album called *I Started Out as A Child*. Guess what? We *all* started out as children. Our childhood experiences may not have been as comical and entertaining as those depicted in jokes, comic strips, cartoons or television programs, but they are ours. Those experiences and memories are what made us who and what we are today.

Our parents, grandparents and caregivers did the very best they could with what they had to work with… their own experiences which shaped and molded them and made them who *they* were. My parents were born in 1926 and 1927. If you are familiar with U.S. history, you have already figured out that they came of age during the great depression. Both my mother and father were surrounded by a consciousness of deprivation and lack. They also had an inner knowing that their destinies were not to spend their entire lives in that poverty and lack.

My father, John Leon Nelson, was born in Luisa, Virginia, in the home of his maternal grandparents. While still a baby, his immediate family which included his parents and older brother migrated to his paternal grandparents' home in Charlotte, North Carolina. When he was about ten or eleven the family relocated once again, this time to Washington, DC. He graduated from Armstrong High School near the end of World War II and was immediately drafted, where he served in the Army Air Corps, the predecessor of what is now the U.S. Air Force. After the end of the war, he worked for a while as a clerk at the Pentagon and in 1948 joined the Washington, DC Fire Department, which at the time was still segregated, with Caucasian officers and African-American firefighters working only in areas populated by people of color. According to my dad, you could almost tell a person's race by their address until the late 1950s to middle 1960s. Of course, there were some exceptions, but they were few and far between.

My mother, Alice Cecelia Chase Nelson, whose grandparents were children when the Emancipation Proclamation was enacted, was born and raised in rural Charles County, Maryland. When my mother was growing up, women of color were fully expected to work as domestics, often leaving their children with family members for weeks at a time. The men worked as farmers on their own property, field hands on someone else's land or in some other position of servitude.

After graduating from high school, my mother escaped from her constrained surroundings and moved in with an aunt in Baltimore where she enrolled in secretarial school. At that time, the notion of an African American secretary was unheard of, but my mother knew her destiny was not to be a Charles County based domestic worker. She worked for a dry cleaner while in secretarial school and upon graduation moved in with another relative in Washington, DC. There, she landed a job as a clerk typist at the Pentagon, where she met my dad. The marriage ultimately ended in divorce, but that's not the point at this juncture.

The point is my parents did all they could to made sure that my brother, Michael, and I never experienced lack of any kind... clothes, private school... cars... the best clothes... cultural enrichment like Broadway plays, the symphony, local theater and all the things they felt would enrich our lives culturally and socially. As a young child, I developed a love of art, ballet and music, especially jazz, classical music and of course rhythm and blues. I even learned to play the flute and piano while in elementary school.

Our parents not only encouraged, but demanded that we have college educations and careers that would sustain us and our families. I got a BS in Business Management from Federal City College [one of three institutions that were combined to become the University of the District of Columbia], and eventually took post graduate courses in both Business Education at Federal City College and Business Administration at Howard University.

Mike earned a degree in Economics from Fisk University in Nashville. The true irony is that both my brother and I are artsy-fartsy and matriculation in Business Management and Economics simply don't fit in with our God-given natures. It's not anybody's fault. Our parents did the very best they could and I believe I speak for Mike as well when I say we will forever be grateful to them for the lessons they taught us.

I speak only for myself, however, when I say if it hadn't been for my parents' encouragement, I would have most likely gotten a degree in literature or liberal arts because I have always loved to write, sketch, paint, sew and sing. I can hear them saying, almost in unison, "You can't make any money as an artist. You need to get a degree in Business Management so you can make some money." Now, I am not entirely sure if they were saying that to make sure I wouldn't be moving in on one of them when I was 35, if they were afraid I'd end up starving in some remote exotic isle, or if it came from their conditioned fear of lack.

At any rate, I acquiesced and got that degree in management. After my brother graduated from Fisk, he immediately went to work as a radio news announcer. I married my son's father at the beginning of my sophomore year at FCC. Our son, Wesley, was born the following April. His dad and I split up shortly after I graduated from FCC and started working as a teacher. I learned quickly that teachers don't really earn enough to support a family alone and flopped around from one boring job to another for a while just to make ends meet.

Eventually, I found my niche in what was then known as Washington's quasi government... a tightly knit network of consultant firms working on federal grants and contracts. I moved fluidly from one firm to another – from one contract to another, and made great professional and personal contacts along the way. I was able to develop my creative talents in ways that I hadn't imagined and still do the nine to five thing in plush surroundings. The conditions, pay and benefits were better than a real government job, except for one thing... that federal pension.

I had actually started out working for the feds when I was still in high school, but left federal service shortly after Wesley was born in order to concentrate on my education and motherhood. In many ways, I found the bureaucracy of working in federal service to be somewhat stifling. I know many people who were able to play the game and survive, but my creative, free spirit would not allow me to seriously consider a lifetime of compromising my personal principles. Needless to say, my bouncing from one job to another every year or so drove my parents up the wall.

My dad often joked about the career paths my brother and I chose saying, "Neither one of my children is working in the field they have their degrees in. Oh well, at least they have an education." Without even being consciously aware of what we were doing, both Michael and I were following our bliss as Joseph Campbell so aptly put it. Our natures, our spirits, told us what we were to do and we eventually followed that, not our conditioning… following the example of our mother when she left the country to become a secretary back in the 1940s. Our mother knew in the depths of her being that a life in Charles County, Maryland, with all of the limitations that people faced there in the 20th Century was not her truth, and she held fast to that truth to the day she died.

Even when we think the things we experience are not for our highest good, everything is always in Divine Order. Our real work is to be open to seeing the truth and receptive to the lessons and blessings that come with each challenge.

As I look back on the many jobs and eclectic work experiences I have had, that degree in business management really did come in handy. Not long after landing in my first job with a consultant firm, I was elevated to administrative manager, supervising a staff, managing budgets, writing grants and reports and reporting directly to federal project managers. My positions made it possible for me to meet many interesting and powerful politicians, entertainers, writers and artists. It was during this phase in my career that I got my first writing credit as part of a team that published two research documents for the Department of Justice.

When federal grant and contract money started to slow down, I went in a completely different direction. After working for a while at Howard University, my love of music led me to WDCU, a university run local public radio station. Many years earlier, I started as a volunteer answering

23

telephones at Pacifica's WPFW during fund-raisers. When I left Howard, I decided to do more of what I truly loved and went to WDCU, run by my alma mater... UDC.

At WDCU, I learned behind the scenes production and on-air techniques. Six months later, the production manager left and I was hired as his replacement. Less than two years after that, I was head of On Air Promotions at NPR's DC headquarters. Without that degree in management, I would not have had the skills or the experience to move so quickly from being a volunteer to production manager at a local public radio station and jump to head of a network department in such a short period of time.

I stayed at NPR until my position was abolished during a reorganization. A few months after leaving NPR, I made good on a promise I made to myself 10 years earlier and moved to a warmer climate. I landed in South Florida and once again reinvented myself, first working in commercial television and ultimately in public affairs, first with community organizations and ultimately with a county government agency. The irony that my career started and ended with government service did not escape me. In fact, I find it quite funny.

My mom passed away in 1999, before I took another gigantic leap of faith, left my second husband, reunited with my soulmate and started taking courses which ultimately led to my becoming an ordained Unity minister. My dad made his transition in 2010. By then I had completed several courses and was well on my way to completing the first of three major steps toward becoming an ordained minister. I had, in fact, put my studies on hold for approximately three years in order to be available for him during his illness and transition.

Growing up and living in the shadow of expectations and beliefs of well-meaning family members and caregivers is not limited to my family. Rev. Toni Boehm, one of my Unity teachers and mentors who has become a friend, shared a story about her own childhood that clearly demonstrates the impact of limiting beliefs and how they can affect a child's self-image. She revealed that from the time she was about four years old, she believed that she could fly and saw herself as being very rich with the ability to turn everything – even the grass and leaves – into money just by wishing it to be. When she was about six years old, she excitedly confided to an uncle that she was really rich. His response was "Oh, honey. You live in Frog Hollow."

After that brief exchange, she never flew again. Her childhood truth was crushed and held prisoner until many years later when she came to realize that the dream of that little girl was in fact a reflection of her true self, not the environment into which she was born and lived.

No doubt, my story and Rev. Toni's story are but two examples among millions or billions where the bright lights of children's dreams and ideas about who and what they are were dimmed or extinguished by people who were incapable of holding that vision along with them.

Imagine what life would be if everyone was allowed to follow their bliss from birth. What would our lives be like if we were guided to be what we were meant to be, not what culture or parents or teachers tell us we are?

> *We live in a culture that uses labels as a means of understanding the world and the people living in it. As a result, many of us find ourselves laboring under a label that has a negative connotation. Unless we can find a way to see the good in such a label, we may feel burdened by an idea of*

ourselves that is not accurate. It is important to remember that almost nothing in this world is all good or all bad, and most everything is a complex mixture of gifts and challenges.

– Daily Om

Exercise 1

What labels are you wearing? Are they your own labels, or are they labels someone else designed for you? What labels do you want to wear? Don't worry about the labels you think you wear right now. Think about the labels you truly want to wear for yourself. Who are you – really? Think about it. Who are you? Take your time. Are you happy wearing these labels? What labels do you want to wear?

Take a few deep relaxing deep breaths and just go with whatever comes to mind. Close your eyes and imagine yourself wearing only the labels you want for yourself. Be as creative and as outlandish as you want to be. What are they? How do they make you feel? If you feel the least bit ill at ease, take another look at the labels. Change them around. Take some off. Add new ones. Nobody can see your labels but you.

THE PERSON YOU CREATE IS THE PERSON YOU TRULY ARE.

CHAPTER 2

So If This Is Who I Truly Am, What Happened?

What happened is we've been wearing the labels society put on us. From the very beginning, our parents label us. "She has her father's nose, her mother's eyes. He has his grandmother's temperament." So do playmates. Consider the nicknames that we heard when we were growing up and possibly even used when addressing our childhood friends. Many of these nicknames some of my peers had remain with them to this very day.

Most of the time, the labels put on us by family and friends are not intended to give us negative feelings about ourselves, but depending on what those labels are, they could have had precisely that effect. The labels assigned to us by teachers and other authority figures are just as potent. I believe I've made my point. My maternal grandmother had a sister who seemed to believe that her life's work was to assign nicknames to every single person in the family. Some of those nicknames were funny. Some were demeaning. There is no doubt that every nickname she bestowed upon one of us was created in love, but some of those names were anything but encouraging... especially for children who might have been dealing with low self-esteem.

I'm not going to take a lot of time talking about the truly negative, hurtful labels people put on each other, because we have all heard them at one time or another, but I must share this example from a real life situation.

In the Washington, DC area, the name Raful Edmond is well known. He is now incarcerated and will likely spend the rest of his life behind bars. This did not have to happen.

His exploits were all over local and national news and naturally the topic of conversation all over the DC metropolitan area. I have no concrete evidence, but given the tragic history of school systems labeling young geniuses as disruptive in traditional classrooms, it is not hard to believe that young Raful was subjected to some unearned harsh criticism and dissolutions while growing up.

In truth, young Raful Edmond was really a genius, and it came to light as he neared adulthood. Unfortunately, he was never able to get rid of the labels he picked up during his childhood. Rather than use his potential and genius to make the world a better place he grew up to become the most notorious drug kingpin the area had ever seen, with a network that rivaled any Fortune 500 company. If when he was an intelligent, energetic child Raful Edmond had been recognized as the genius that he was, there's no telling what good he could have done in the world.

I can't help but wonder how many geniuses are languishing in prison or worse because their true spirits were never recognized, and eventually broken by the weight of labels that denied their divine gifts. What child could sit quietly in a boring traditional first or second grade class day after day when they are light years beyond the rest of the class?

We should all be highly concerned about the number of today's children who are labeled ADHD and sedated just to maintain order in a classroom. Our education system needs to be looked at very, very closely. Too many of our children's lives... and their spirits... are being destroyed by a structure that thrives on placing negative labels on innocent, vulnerable children. Schools in the 21st Century are nothing more than mills where our children are trained to pass tests. Children are denied the educations that they deserve.

Administrators and teachers are forced to concentrate their energies on reaching 'measurable outcomes' in order to satisfy the bean counters who came up with the notion of subjecting children to stress inducing standardized testing, leaving precious little room for a child whose learning style does not conform with the prescribed method du jour. Children who cannot measure up are automatically relegated to the ominous categories of unteachable, slow learner, special needs, or worse. The most egregious acts include punishing naturally curious children by labeling them as having Asperger's Syndrome or full-blown ADHD. Medicating children and shuttling them into a classroom situation where they are told that they are incapable of functioning in the world is, in my opinion, criminal. There are, no doubt, hyperactive children who certainly do require special attention. However, I suspect that many of the youngsters who have been identified as having 'special needs' are really geniuses who are in need of a more challenging classroom experience or simply learn in ways different from the methods used in the classroom.

Had I been in a traditional classroom today, I would almost certainly be in one of those special needs classes. All the way through high school and in college, was never able to perform mathematical and algebraic formulae the way they were taught in my classes. I did, however, almost always come up with the correct answer. On tests and examinations where only the correct answer was considered, I always scored above average. However, when I was put to the task of showing how I arrived at my answers, my grades suffered. During my sophomore year in college, I participated in a research project that determined that I am mildly dyslexic. The blessing in this is that no one was doing this kind of research when I was in elementary school. Otherwise, I would have been saddled with a label that would have interfered with my entire life. What real difference does it make if I sometimes reverse my lowercase d's and b's, occasionally get a telephone number wrong or create my own method for solving mathematical equations? It works for me and no one complains. Besides, if they did complain who would really care?

About five years after my introduction to New Thought and the Unity movement, I shared my dyslexia story with a man I had been dating for about six months. One of the reasons that relationship did not last was his insistence that I accept that my ability to learn and perceive things differently was a 'disability'. My refusal to take on the 'disabled' label proved to be a pivotal moment in that brief association as well as in my own perception of myself. I had never considered the gift of seeing things differently to be anything less than a blessing. His adamant insistence that there was something wrong with anyone who could perceive something in a manner other than what he determined to be normal was very telling. In my opinion, he was making a concerted effort to see me as less than perfect. Although I was a relative neophyte in terms of New Thought and Unity, I knew enough to withhold permission from anyone to alter my self-image in a way that is not in alignment with the divine being that I am. Armed with this wisdom, it was my choice to accept or reject this new label and my responsibility to do the work necessary to eradicate it from my consciousness.

We are all given labels as we go through life. While we may have been able to toss some of these labels aside along the way, others are thrown our way almost every day. We just got rid of some during the exercise at the end of Chapter 1.

So here we are with all these new labels that keep coming our way. But let's be honest... with each new label, we are still laboring under some of the old mindsets created by those which were recently discarded. It is up to us to erase the subliminal messages implanted by years of unhealthy conditioning. The first thing we have to do is deny that those definitions and attributes have any place in our lives – deny that we have any of those character traits. Next, we must affirm that we are who we know we are as identified by the labels we selected earlier.

In first Corinthians, Paul wrote that the resurrected nature of Christ in man is the mystery that has been hidden for generations. He described it as our 'hope of glory.' That's precisely what we're dealing with here. For generations, humankind has been laboring under the mistaken assumption that God is outside of us. As children of God, we have inherited infinite spiritual attributes the same way we inherited our physical parents' eyes, blood type, nose and bone structure. It is our responsibility to recognize that if we claim to be children of God, we are perfect in every way.

Denials and affirmations are used to clear away old, negative habits and beliefs that no longer serve us. Affirmations are positive statements, attitudes and beliefs that replace those things that stand in our way and restrict our ability to achieve our highest good. It is important to remember that affirmations alone, while they may work in the short term, have no long-lasting power without first clearing away limiting thoughts with denials. When denials and affirmations are used together, old thought patterns are eradicated and new, prospering beliefs become embedded in our consciousness and therefore bring about permanent change in our subconscious mind.

Let us here and now DENY that we are difficult to get along with, lazy, stupid, incapable of having any happiness, or that we are unlovable and AFFIRM that we are affable, energetic, intelligent, joyful and lovable.

Exercise 2

Before starting this exercise, let's take a look at an example of how to write our own denials and affirmations:

Denial: This situation has no affect upon my personal circumstances.

Affirmation: All things are working together for my highest good.

Take a few minutes to do your own denials and affirmations... permanently shedding those labels you don't want and using super glue to attach the labels that truly identify you as the person you really are. Repeat this exercise as often as you like – whenever and wherever you like. Write your denials and affirmations down. Tape them to your mirror, your dashboard, your computer monitor at home and at work.

Repeat these denials and affirmations at least two or three times a day. Unwanted labels come to us all the time. It is our responsibility to ourselves to constantly remove and replace them with the labels we want... to strive to be the person we know God intended us to be... the person that God knows we already are.

I AM AS GOD CREATED ME!

CHAPTER 3

Love Yourself

*Love does not delight in evil but rejoices with
the truth. It always protects, always trusts,
always hopes, always perseveres.*

– 1 Corinthians 13: 6-7

The first real step toward realizing true prosperity is
to LOVE YOURSELF. Every time you look into a mirror,
walk past one or even when you catch a glimpse of your own
eyes as you adjust the mirrors in your car, say "I love you!"
It may feel funny at first, but do it anyway. God loves you,
so why shouldn't you love yourself?

I love myself so much
That I can love you so much
That you can love you so much
That you can start loving me
– Richard Medeci

The lyrics to that little song say it all. It's impossible
to love someone else before you can love yourself. Lack of
self-love leads to low self-esteem, acceptance of abuse,
cruelty and the belief that unhappiness and dissatisfaction
are normal. This is not God's plan for us. If we just take a
moment to think about it, we would recognize that the truth
was always with us. As little children, we were taught to
sing, "Jesus loves me this I know for the bible tells me so…"
Since we were told as three and four year olds that we have
the unconditional love of Jesus, why is low self-esteem such
a problem? I contend that many of the messages in the
bible… especially those that conveyed beliefs in
unworthiness… were not only distorted by those charged

with translating the original Hebrew, Greek and Aramaic scriptures through the centuries, but also by erroneous interpretation, honest mistakes made during translation and transcription and sometimes outright manipulation. This happened for a variety of reasons.

One of the main reasons the original texts were manipulated was the desire to control the masses. Whenever people have access to and full understanding of the true message – that we are one with the universe and that everyone has a birthright of divinity from God – there is no need for political leadership, corporate dependency or fear of any kind. This is the nexus of the Gnostic teachings. I won't go into detail about the persecution of Gnostics here, but I will say that Gnosticism is, in my opinion, more closely aligned with the teachings of Jesus than traditional religious theology and dogma. If you are interested in delving into this theory, and the history of Gnosticism and its relationship with traditional Christianity, check out some of the many books on the history of early Christianity and Gnosticism by Elaine Pagels and others.

How can we be expected to love our neighbor as ourselves, as Jesus taught in Matthew 22:39, if we do not love ourselves?

This is one of the biggest oxymorons of traditional Christian teachings one can imagine. It is clear that Jesus was telling the Pharisees and all who were present that it is impossible for us to love anyone before we love ourselves. We must love ourselves unconditionally, just as God created us – without judgment or recrimination for any of our traits, tendencies or preferences. Looking into the mirror and saying "I love you" to yourself is one of the best ways to start the process of eradicating the old teachings and removing labels that convey the error message that we are not worthy of love. Learning to love and accept ourselves is the very best way to get rid of low self-esteem, which is at the root of many if not all addictions, obsessions and fears.

Once we understand that we are worthy of unconditional love, loving ourselves and others becomes easy.

Exercise 3

In addition to looking into mirrors and saying "I love you," commit to a daily practice of engaging in at least three of the self-care activities below.

1. Pamper yourself. Treat yourself like royalty. It doesn't have to be anything super extravagant or expensive. Take a long, relaxing bubble bath. Light candles, play some soft music and just linger in the tub until you turn into a prune. ☺ Get a massage and/or a facial. Take yourself out to dinner or fix your favorite meal. If you are at home, use the good dishes... the ones you save for company. More on that below.

2. Pick one:
   a. Take a walk in a park or at the beach.
   b. Go for a drive in the country.
   Whichever you choose, make sure you go all alone and just enjoy your own company.

3. Stop saving the good stuff for company. I can't count the number of people I know who have luxurious towels hanging in their powder rooms. These elaborate items are décor embellishments only while plain or decorative disposable paper towels are provided for the nasty work of drying one's hands. All the while, threadbare linen is designated for day to day use by the occupants. Did you grow up in a home where the 'good china' was never used except for holidays and major events, like weddings or funerals? Why not use the good stuff to celebrate life's little triumphs? Birthdays... good report cards... a good report from the doctor... a new job... a child's appearance in a school play or winning a

basketball or football game. These are all cause for celebration. Break out the good stuff and use it any time you get the urge. It's a known fact that crystal that sits on a shelf and collects dust becomes brittle and shatters much more easily than crystal that is used. The oil from our hands helps strengthen it and makes it more durable. I have four sets of dishes. They are all my 'every day' dishes, because at any time, I may decide that the fabulously beautiful red snapper dinner I prepared on a Saturday was worthy of the 24 carat gold trimmed Noritake... and I put it in the dishwasher! I have always hated washing dishes and don't waste time or energy washing anything in my kitchen by hand. The only exceptions are those things that are hand painted and cast iron cookware.

4. Your home really *is* your castle. Make sure your home is inviting and comfortable to you. Why clean up for company and live in a pigsty the rest of the time? Even if you live in a one room studio apartment, whenever you walk into your own home, you should feel welcomed and happy to be there. Your sleeping area should be a very special haven of peace, love and tranquility. When you rest, you should always be able to rest your body and your mind. Get rid of the clutter. Hang up your clothes. Put the laundry in the hamper. As I sit here writing this, I must confess that I too must change a bad habit. I love to read, and that includes reading in bed. When my companion is at home, it's not a problem, because I keep my 'bedroom' books in or on the chest at the foot of the bed. But whenever he goes out of town, those books slowly fill up his

side of the bed. Waking up to a bed full of books is not my idea of an inviting good morning kiss. If you are a bed reader like me, train yourself to put that book or magazine on the nightstand when you reach over to turn off the light.

5. Do little things to make your home inviting to yourself and your guests. Treat yourself like company. One of my friends keeps a basket on the counter of her guest bathroom filled with white washcloths. These cloths are soft and fresh for drying hands or for freshening up. On the floor is a linen lined basket here the washcloths are disposed of. Depending upon how much company she has on any given day, the washcloths are cleaned and dried and neatly placed back in that basket. This is a wonderful way to encourage guests to remember that they, too, are lovable and loved... and that they are truly worthy of self-love. Every time she uses her own guest bathroom, she, too, is reminded that she is loved and lovable. Another friend places huge silk flowers on her bed and the bed of her guest room. Before going to bed every night, she and her guests are treated to a beautiful bouquet of flowers. In my own house, my ongoing gift to myself and my guests is aroma therapy. Not the stuff you plug in which tends to trigger allergic reactions in a lot of people – myself included, but tiny baskets of natural potpourri all over the place.

6. Get a hobby. Engage in an activity that gives you personal and emotional pleasure at least once a week. Pick something that does not necessarily involve a television or another individual. Some

people enjoy playing video games or reading. Others get pleasure from cooking or just listening to music. Still others are extroverts and are only truly energized by being in the presence of others. These people are most happy when engaging in activities that involve the participation of other people. For extroverts, I recommend team sports, tennis, racquet ball and things of that sort. Extroverts who are not particularly excited about participating in high energy sports activities could become involved with community organizations, clubs and groups which share common interests.

7. Take care of your body temple. Walk, jog, exercise, yoga. Everything in moderation… we hear it all the time, but few of us really adhere to his sage advice. Limit your meat, dairy, sugar and alcohol intake. Eat your veggies and fresh fruit. Back away from the buffet and make fewer trips to the dessert tray. Schedule regular check-ups with your dentist, primary care doctor and eye care specialist; and make sure you get plenty of rest.

This is just a short list of self-care activities that help enhance your quality of life. It could go on ad infinitum, but you get the idea. You deserve the very best.

LOVE YOURSELF ENOUGH TO TAKE GOOD CARE OF YOURSELF AND DO IT EVERY DAY!

CHAPTER 4

Let It Go

It's up to us to recognize that everyone is following their own individual path and while our paths cross the paths of millions of others, their journeys are not our journeys. In other words, their burdens are not ours to bear. Their mistakes are not ours to correct. Their faults are not ours to remedy. Their problems are not ours to solve.

There's no way we can realize our own spiritual greatness if we are constantly trying to control the people around us. This applies to everyone - especially our spouses and our children. We are in relationship with our partners and spouses to learn, to grow and to nurture... not to change. If anyone enters into a relationship with another individual with the notion that they can change or fix another, the relationship is doomed from the very beginning – even if it endures several years.

As parents, we are responsible for guiding and nurturing our children. Parents are responsible for teaching, not controlling their children. In his book, *The Prophet*, Kahlil Ghibran wrote:

> *"Your children are not your children.*
> *They are the sons and daughters of Life's longing for itself.*
> *They come through you but not from you,*
> *And though they are with you yet they belong not to you.*
> *You may give them your love but not your thoughts,*
> *For they have their own thoughts.*

You may house their bodies but not their
souls
For their souls dwell in the house of
tomorrow, which you cannot visit not even in
your dreams.
You may strive to be like them, but seek not to
make them like you.
For life goes not backward nor tarries with
yesterday.
You are the bows from which your children's
living arrows are sent forth.
The archer [God] sees the mark upon the
path of the infinite, and he bends you with His
might that His arrows may go swift and far.
Let your bending in the archer's hand be for
gladness;
For even as He loves the arrow that flies, so
He loves also that bow that is stable."

If we are not supposed to control our children, then who is responsible for controlling these little beings? The answer is simple. Nobody. No one on the face of this planet has the authority to control another person. This doesn't mean we are not responsible for obeying laws or procedures or teaching our children to obey the laws of the land. What it means is no one has the right or the power to control the ideas, destiny or spiritual calling of another.

My personal theory is that people are prone to depression, violence, physical and emotional illness when they are denied their God-given birthright to follow their own path by well-meaning parents, teachers, significant others and authority figures, as well as some whose intentions are obviously not in their best interests.

When driving, we are all bound by traffic laws. When you accept a job, you are responsible for following all the rules and regulations of the workplace. If for whatever reason you do not agree with those rules and regulations, you have the freedom to change jobs. In fact, you have a spiritual obligation to remove yourself from any situation that does not fulfill your personal mission for being on this earth. Remaining in an unhealthy work environment will result in physical and emotional distress.

Anyone who has known me for more than a few years will attest to the fact that I have adhered to this personal rule of thumb for most of my professional life. There have been a few instances when the money was so good, or the benefits were so phenomenal that I tried to ride it out. On those rare occasions when I did not pay attention to my own inner voice, I either became physically ill or was so stressed out that I was eventually forced to leave the job and all of the money and perks behind for my own personal well-being. How many people are you aware of who allow their jobs to ruin their health or destroy relationships? I am personally aware of two people who literally died on the job.

Again – my personal theory is that the reason for so many cases of hypertension, chronic pain, diabetes, and the like is the body's way of telling us to change something in our lives… be it a job, a toxic relationship, a long-time habit or a complete change in life-style. Accidents are also God's way of teaching us lessons.

In the fall of 1993, I was extremely busy at work at home and socially. While meditating, God distinctly told me to 'slow down.' Smart alec that I am, I said to God, "I know I need to slow down, and I will just as soon as I finish x, y, and z." Well, the first thing God did to try to get my attention was manifested in the form of severe muscle spasms which landed me in the hospital for three days, and confined to my home for another week.

I was living in Washington, DC at the time and the annual Congressional Black Caucus started the very day I was cleared by my physician. Anxious to get involved in all the festivities, I called a family member and together we made arrangements to go a Capitol Hill jazz concert that evening. She picked me up at the appointed time, but we hadn't gone more than two blocks from my apartment building when we were rear-ended. I was diagnosed with a compression fracture in my lower spine. I spent a month in bed walked with a cane for nearly a year and spent more than a full year with a physical therapist. Needless to say, I learned my lesson. Regardless of what may be going on in my life now, when God tells me to slow down, I immediately apply the brakes, no matter who or what is disrupted by my sudden decision to shift gears or to completely back away from a situation altogether.

At times, shifting gears or changing direction can be disruptive to the people around you. Doing so may even be initially disruptive to your own life, but if you follow your spirit, you will always come out ahead of the game. The bottom line is always be true to yourself and to your own spirit, and encourage those around you to do the same. Mutual respect and unconditional love are the orders of the day.

Earlier in this chapter, I referred to toxic relationships. It is essential that we recognize the signs of toxicity in a relationship and take steps to put space between ourselves and friends, relatives or loved ones who are negative influences or do not encourage us to be the persons we were meant to be. Emotional blackmail, co-dependency and physical, verbal or emotional abuse are all clear indicators of toxic relationships. If faced with any one of these, make haste! They are blocking your blessings.

Take inventory of your relationships. Are you blocking someone's blessings through your own actions or reactions to their dreams? Is someone blocking your blessings? If so, then let go. Regardless of how long you've been in the situation or what you may believe, letting go is best for both of you. No one can reach their highest good if they are being held hostage by any form of emotional blackmail from another individual. In some recovery circles, it's called co-dependency or enabling. Passive aggressiveness is another emotional weapon that is used to control the actions of others. Regardless of what it's called, the bottom line is the same – people tend to use emotional weapons to control others or coerce them into doing something that is in complete opposition to their highest good.

We must recognize when we are being targeted by others to act in ways that are not in our best interest. It is also critical to remember that we, too, can overstep our boundaries and use emotional blackmail on others. Therefore, we must once again look into that mirror and know when we are guilty of using emotional blackmail on others.

Exercise 4

Take inventory of your emotions:

- How do you feel upon waking up in the morning?
- Do you look forward to going to work? Whether your answer is 'yes' or 'no' why do you feel the way you do about your job? Is it fulfilling on the intangible level?
- Do you have harmonious relationships with the people around you?
- What if anything would you change and why?
- What is keeping you from doing the things you truly want to do with your day?
- Are your happiness and self-worth tied to the opinions and reactions of others? Why?
- How can your relationships be more fulfilling?
- Are the people in your life supportive of your dreams?
- Why are you holding onto those things that no longer serve your highest good?
- What would your life look like if you released everything that no longer serves you?
- What are you doing to block the blessings of others?
- Why are you engaging in this activity?
- Why are you unwilling to release your attachment to the outcomes of others?
- What steps can you take to release this attachment and trust God, allowing the highest good to unfold? In other words… why won't you get out of the way?

LET GO AND LET GOD!!!

CHAPTER 5

Forgive and Forget

"I forgive all condemnation that I misperceived to be mine. I give understanding for that condemnation. I am set free to live in the Christ Spirit by the quality of my forgiveness."
  – *Stretton Smith 4T Prosperity Program*

Forgive and forget. Easier said than done, but necessary for our sake more than the sake of the people we believe have offended us.

How many times have we repeated The Lord's Prayer by rote and never gave any thought to the true meaning of what we've been saying all these years? Have you sincerely considered the words... "Forgive us our trespasses as we forgive those who trespass against us."? Do you have any idea what that means? In plain English, it means, "Dear God, forgive me for my error thoughts and deeds the same way I forgive people who have I perceived to have offended me." In many cases, it's our perception of wrongdoing that creates the illusion of injury. *A Course in Miracles* goes so far as to say that everything is an illusion, and as such, nothing is real – not even the worst of situations.

That concept is often difficult to comprehend, and I won't attempt to go into a detailed dialog on that theory here, but in a nutshell... we can't take everything done by others as our personal burden. It'll weigh us down and we'll end up drowning in anger, self-pity and hatred. Before long, all this negative energy will result in physical illness and we'll wonder what in the world happened to our bodies.

In fact, Don Miguel Ruiz identified it as the first of his *Four Agreements*... "Don't take it personally". People have destroyed their entire lives, holding grudges and being angry with others... sometimes without even knowing why. The most well-known is probably the decades long feud between the Hatfields and the McCoys or to bring it even closer to home... the Civil War.

In the 21st Century, we are still dealing with debates and fervor over confederate flags, statues and images of confederate generals – even in the sanctuary of the National Cathedral in our nation's capital. At the conclusion of the revolutionary war and the war of 1812, there were no honors or tributes paid to the British. No icons of Spain were given places of honor in this country after the Spanish-American War. The confederacy was defeated more than 150 years ago, yet confederate iconography still holds places of honor on state property throughout the southern US.

This anger has festered into a malignancy that continues to haunt every American citizen. It is this malignancy that I suspect is at the root of all the racial, economic and class conflicts that we are experiencing all across this country.

A prime example of how serious this malignancy really is was unveiled during the 2016 presidential election in the US and continues to this very day. Its outcome, the reactions of Americans and the international community are reverberating all around us. The things said and done by the 45th president are in my opinion, a direct result of what happens when you allow the malignancy of unforgiveness to go unchecked for many decades.

The people who revered the confederacy and all of the horror and pain that it represents since the 1800s are the ancestors of the people who threw stones, bombs and used water hoses on the freedom fighters of the 1960s. They and their descendants are now re-emboldened to act out in horrific ways against women, minorities and Muslims in this country and abroad. This malignancy will continue to fester until all of us – regardless of which side of the debate you stand on – take serious active participation in real forgiveness work.

Martin Luther King, Jr., taught love, unconditional love and forgiveness. I have no doubt that had he survived that 1968 shooting in Memphis, he would have forgiven the persons responsible for his death just as he forgave the individual who stabbed him in 1958 and the many people who stoned, hit and attacked him before his assassination.

Nearly every Unity service ends with those in attendance joining hands and singing *Let There Be Peace on Earth*. The closing line is "... and let it begin with me". Peace and forgiveness is an individual thing and universal peace starts with each individual.

Anger is an emotion that many of us unknowingly turn on ourselves. Not forgiving ourselves for things we are often not even aware of is one of the most damaging things we can do. We must learn to forgive ourselves for mistakes and perceived wrong-doing, even if we did those things willingly and with full knowledge of their consequences. We must accept the fact that we were influenced by feelings and emotions that prompted us to do the things that we are now feeling guilty about.

Forgiving oneself isn't easy, but we must at all times remember that we did the best that we could at the time. Even if we 'knew better,' for whatever reason, we did the very best we could in that exact circumstance, at that particular time and in that specific place. It is very important to know at the deepest level of our being that in God's eyes, all is already forgiven. God loves us unconditionally. With God, there is nothing to forgive. We take on a sense of guilt because we allow others to make us feel guilty and because we have condemned ourselves.

> *When you express approval of yourself or others, you are glorifying the divine in yourself and others.*

> – *Catherine Ponder; The Prospering Power of Love*

Exercise 5

Sit in a quiet place with a notebook. Open it so that two blank pages are facing you. Draw a line down the middle of both pages. On the page to the left, make a list of all the people you think have offended or hurt you in the left column. In the left column of the page on the right, make a list of all the people *you* have offended or hurt.

Back to the page on your left-hand side, write a short description of what each person did to offend or hurt in the column next to their names. Now move over to the page where you have listed the people you hurt and or offended. Make a list of all the things for which you need forgiveness. Take as long as you need. Use as much paper as necessary.

Once your lists are complete, rip them from your notebook and flip to two clean pages. Looking at the list of people who hurt you, write the words "I FORGIVE" and then write the name of the first person on your list and whatever you have in the column next to their name. Do this for each person on your list and then do the same thing with the list of people you hurt or offended. Now, throw away the first lists and take your forgiveness lists into meditation.

Keep them in a very special, private place. Anytime you want to beat yourself up about something from the past, remind yourself that you love yourself and everyone in your life unconditionally and have already forgiven them and yourself for past errors and error thoughts.

AS I FORGIVE, I AM FORGIVEN.

CHAPTER 6
Back Away From the Television

...when there is a painful, fearful, anxious, or hateful thought or feeling in your mind -- so that you look out and see a world that is painful, hateful, or fearful...
– Guy Finley

Years ago, sociologists revealed that by the time our children graduate from high school, they would have seen hundreds of thousands of simulated murders on television and in movies. How many times have children imitated death scenes, either as victim or perpetrator to the applause and approval of family and friends? Is there any wonder that violence prevails in almost every aspect of our lives?

Someone said that a violent scene is televised in the United States every 38 seconds. Add to that the daily onslaught of murders in the daily news, we are all traumatized by violent death everywhere we turn. One sure way to bring peace into our lives is to very carefully monitor what we and especially our children are exposed to on television.

Programs and even channels that offer a lot of violence or destruction as entertainment should be blocked as well as movies and television programs that denigrate women or any other segment of society. These shows anesthetize us and subliminally condition us to accept negative stereotypes and attitudes as normal and acceptable. An added side effect of repeated exposure to simulated and actual acts of violence is a constant feeling of fear and insecurity. Watching scenes depicting graphic violence of all kinds has made us afraid to walk out the door. I know one woman who is not only afraid to leave her home, she is fearful of even looking out the window. Every window in her home is shuttered tight... keeping out all daylight and any opportunity to see what she perceives as the fearful, scary outside world.

Thoughts held in mind produce after their kind. The law of attraction is always at work. One of the primary lessons in *The Secret* is what we think about is what we get in life. If we are fearful of anything, we bring more fear into our lives. If you really want peace, stop watching movies about war. Limit the amount of time you spend watching, reading and listening to the news of the day. If it's in your consciousness, it will be in your life.

Think about the daily news. Is it really necessary to start your day with the news? Are the latest celebrity gossip, political scandal, the declining economy, war and threat of war the way to start a bright, happy, peaceful day? Does it really matter if you are aware of every detail of each political debate congressional inquiry? Why is it necessary for us to be immersed in conversation about the most recent aberration committed by a national leader.

How do you feel after coming home from a long stressful day at work and horrific traffic jams to two or three hours of televised news every evening? I challenge you to take a break from the news at least one day a week. Believe it or not, the Earth won't leave its axis if you miss the bombardment of scandal, death, destruction, murder and mayhem every once in a while.

Pay special attention to how you feel when you go to bed at the end of your news boycott day. Chances are you will rest better and feel more invigorated in the morning. Not only is it impossible to go through life without being aware of current events, it's irresponsible, but it's not necessary to eat, drink, sleep, live and breathe the day's news. One local newspaper and one hour of television and/or radio news per day should be sufficient.

I personally try to keep it down to 30 minutes per day. In all honesty, though, with everything that's going on in the world these days, it is practically impossible to strictly adhere to that 30 minute rule. I do, however, keep it under 60 minutes and abstain from all news early in the morning, before I go to bed and at mealtime. Starting and ending your day in a peaceful frame of consciousness is essential to maintaining balance and harmony. Eating while watching or listening to newscasts can easily set the stage for digestive problems, ulcers, heartburn, increased blood pressure and challenges with blood sugar levels going awry.

Next, check the television shows and movies you're watching. Does what you watch reflect the world in which you want to live? What about the music you listen to at various times during your day? Is the music you choose to expose your consciousness to uplifting, calming or do you find it to be disturbing to your sense of peace and serenity? Does the entertainment you select stir feelings of anxiety or fear?

I used to read the New York Times, Washington Post, and USA Today just about every day. In the evening, I watched two hours of local news, thirty minutes of network news and then switched to CNN and back to local news at 10 or 11. Add the fact that I was working at National Public Radio's Washington, DC headquarters and I had rapidly turned into a real news junkie. It helped that I was also working part time as a fill-in disc jockey at a local radio station, which provided a little bit of distraction from my day-in day-out news routine.

Thankfully, I had begun studying spirituality and metaphysics and started making efforts to put some balance in my life. The first thing I did was get rid of my wristwatch.

At work, everything was timed to the tenth of a second, but once I left work, it didn't matter what time it was, so why bother? By limiting the amount of time I spent watching news programs, eliminating the wristwatch and changing my TV and movie viewing habits, I soon discovered a heightened level of serenity in my home and my life.

Why not seek out radio stations and television programming that enriches your life spiritually and intellectually? It isn't necessary to limit your entertainment to classical music or PBS and The Learning Channel in order to change your world. Take an inventory of what you expose yourself to. Pay attention to story lines and program descriptions before tuning in. Most of us have access to either cable or satellite television. With hundreds of channels to choose from, there's always something on that does NOT depict acts of violence, hatred and fear. Let's make it a priority to find them. The really good news is I have discovered that even without cable, satellite or internet television, we can access some very interesting and enlightening television selections.

Disgusted with mounting satellite and cable television bills, I set about seeking more cost-effective alternatives. Currently, there are three televisions in my home. Only one is connected to a cable service. One is equipped with a simple antenna which gives us access to far more channels and choices than I imagined possible. Several of these channels are not even available on cable or satellite in my part of the country. We get programming through a wi-fi service on the third television, giving us access to almost limitless entertainment sources. We are now seriously considering releasing the cable connection and replacing it with another wi-fi unit.

The very last of Wayne Dyer's, *Ten Secrets for Success and Inner Peace*, teaches us that *"Wisdom is avoiding all thoughts that weaken you."* Constant exposure to destructive thoughts and messages, overt or subliminal, only serve to weaken our spirits, our minds and eventually our bodies.

Exercise 6

Pick a day of the week when you will not watch, listen to or read any news. Do this as a permanent part of your routine. Take one news boycott day every single week for the rest of your life. Even though it may be a challenge, avoid discussing current events with others during your news boycott day as well.

It may be too difficult for some people to just quit the news cold turkey. For those people, I suggest you start by limiting yourself to sixty then thirty minutes of television or radio news. Reduce the amount of time you devote to the news each week until you have totally eliminated your exposure to the news for one full day each week.

While you're weaning yourself from the news, sit down with a red felt tip pen, a highlighter and a printout of the television listings available to you. Highlight all of the programs you watch on a daily and/or weekly basis. Once you've done that, use the red pen to ex out all of the shows that depict violence, degradation, negativity or promote fear of anything or anyone. What's left on your highlighted list?

Now read through the program listings again. This time, use the red felt tip pen to circle shows that you have never watched before. Before circling anything however, take time to read the storylines. Do they offer new information, opportunities to expand your mind, enhance your creativity or enrich your spirit?

TUNE IN AND GET READY TO GROW.

I HONOR MY TRUTH.

I AM AS GOD CREATED ME.

CHAPTER 7

You Already Have All You That You Will Ever Need

We can either spend our time thinking about what we <u>don't</u> have, feeling empty and bitter over some imagined contentment lost... or we can become quietly aware of what we already <u>are</u> and find there, within our Self, what is overflowing, full of Light, and beyond the reach of any dark thought.

– Guy Finley

God has already given us everything we will ever need to be happy in life. It's up to us to take the blinders off and welcome his blessings into our lives.

What we want to achieve is within us. We've all heard the saying "If you dream it, you can achieve it." There is absolutely nothing wrong with wanting – or even having – money, cars, homes, clothes... whatever your personal dream may be. God gives us those dreams. It's our job to accept them as our reality and live them out. We seldom know exactly how to live out our dreams, but that's where prayer and meditation come in.

In *The Secret*, we're reminded that when we're driving on the highway at night, our headlights illumine only the next few yards ahead of us. That's all we need to see at that particular time. We don't worry about what's beyond that few yards because we know that as we drive along the road, our headlights will show us next few yards and the next until we reach our destination. We must have that same kind of faith when going after our dreams.

If you're in a situation where your funds are limited, but you want to travel around the world, just get a passport and know that doors will open for you to see the world. Who knows? You may find yourself employed in the airline industry or in some other position that requires you to travel extensively in the performance of your duties. It happens. In fact, it happened to me.

In the very early pages of this book, I talked about my history of job hopping. When I first graduated from college, I worked as a teacher. I was a single mom and all my resources went to maintaining a stable home for my son and me. Not long after I filed for divorce, without any conscious knowledge of spirituality and metaphysics, I decided I wanted to see as much of the US as I possibly could.

In just a few weeks, I landed a job with American Express Travel Division. Although the pay was better, the job itself was completely monotonous and boring. I didn't stay there long. Being in that environment really gave the travel bug a chance to settle in. For the next eight years, I bounced from one consultant firm to another, traveling all over the United States, doing whatever my job description called for... managing conferences... conducting trainings... setting up and managing seminars... attending workshops.

I traveled first class, stayed in the best hotels, ate the finest food and visited places I would never have been able to get to if I had to pay for everything myself. I was even able to take my son on some of those trips. It was a wonderfully eye-opening experience for both of us. Looking back, I came to understand how much I limited myself by just wanting to see the US. Had I held a broader vision, I would have, indeed, been able to travel the entire globe in the performance of my duties.

In the book, *Prosperity*, Unity co-founder, Charles Fillmore wrote:

> *It is perfectly logical to assume that a wise and competent Creator would provide for the needs of His creatures in their various stages of growth. The supply that would be given as required and as the necessary effort for its appropriation was made by the creature. Temporal needs would be met by temporal things. Mental needs be things of like character, and spiritual needs by spiritual elements.*

By today's standards, the language is stilted and antiquated, but his message is one that cannot be ignored. The bigger your faith, the bigger the miracles God works in your life. You hold the key. Unlock the gates.

Exercise 7

This exercise is going to be fun.

Take out your journal and sit quietly for a few minutes thinking about all the times you wanted something to manifest in your life and it came to you. Pay special attention to those things that came to you from a completely unexpected source. Perhaps it was just a telephone call or a visit from someone special in your life. Or, maybe it was a particular item of clothing, or an opportunity to attend a social gathering. No matter how large or small, write it down.

Now, imagine something big that you want... something that you want to do or see manifest in your life.

Write it down.

See it as if it has already happened. Act as though it is already yours and go on with your daily routine.

After 24 hours, go back to your journal. This time, write about how it feels to have your wish fulfilled. How does it affect your five senses? What does it look like? Is there a smell associated with your wish – or a taste? What about sounds? What are they? Can you touch it? Is it smooth to the touch? Soft? Hard? Rough? Wet?

Be as specific as you can. Write it all down in as much detail as you possibly can. Then release it to the universe.

As a supplement to your journal entry, create a vision board. Vision boards or treasure maps are excellent tools to use when creating a new reality. If you have never made a vision board, you might at first think that it is an exercise in child's play. In a way, it is. Most children daydream and create within their imaginations the world and lives of their dreams – often remembering things that they experienced in the spirit realm before taking on human form.

Before you begin, gather the following supplies:

- Poster board

- Glue stick

- Magazines

- Scissors

- Optional supplies

    o Glitter

    o Crayon or colored marking pens

    o Stickers

Set aside a few hours of uninterrupted time. Before assembling your vision board, spend time in the silence, meditating, seeking guidance from Holy Spirit, affirming that you will be guided to create the life that is right and perfect for you and for your highest good as well as the highest good of any individual who you might include in your vision.

If you create a vision board or treasure map properly, you will discover that the process is extremely cathartic. Combining journaling with visioning your dreams is far more powerful than journaling alone or taking time to create a vision board without journaling about your dreams and desires.

When the things that you visualize and journal about come to you as a physical manifestation, don't be surprised. There are no coincidences. The third Unity principle teaches us that we are co-creators with God. You and God working together in harmony bring all of your experiences into physical reality. Why not use these gifts to create the things and circumstances that you truly desire?

God works miracles in our lives even when we're not paying attention, but when we focus on God's greatness and open ourselves up to lovingly accepting the gifts God has in store for us, we can achieve anything and everything our hearts desire.

I AM PROSPEROUS!!!

CHAPTER 8

There's Plenty to Go Around

... if we desire much joy and happiness, we must radiate more happiness into the lives of others.

– Georgiana Tree West – Prosperity's 10 Commandments

As responsible stewards of the gifts God bestows upon us, it is essential that we share our blessings. There are plenty of opportunities for us to share our time, treasure and talents. Just look around.

It's wonderful to see people jump onto planes, trains, and buses and fly to devastated areas in the aftermath of a crises like widespread wildfires, Hurricane Katrina and earthquakes in Haiti and the midwestern US. Most of us have been moved by the outpouring of support for victims of mass shootings and attacks that unfortunately occur with far too much frequency across the globe. Let us not forget that homeless shelters, senior citizens' centers, food pantries, and any number of local charities need help each and every day.

This is not to diminish the need of the victims of natural disasters or attacks upon large numbers of innocent people. Many of my own relatives were displaced by Hurricane Katrina, and our family is eternally grateful for the aid they received after that devastating storm. My point is we should not wait until a catastrophe is brought to the forefront of our consciousness via 24-hour television coverage to take action.

The Bible teaches us to bring our tithes to the storehouse. It is our duty to tithe to the source from which we are spiritually fed. It is our duty to offer our gifts to our communities. Withholding our time, tithe and talents is tantamount to being the spoiled brat who takes and takes everything they can get their hands on while making constant unrealistic demands upon everyone in their circle without any consideration for the needs of siblings, other family members or playmates.

Bill Gates, Warren Buffett and George Soros are but a few prime examples of people who not only share their time, tithe and talent. Yes; they have plenty to share, but so did people like Bernie Madoff, who is serving a life sentence for a massive Ponzi scheme that bankrupted hundreds of people.

Whether we agree with government intervention for the segments of our society who are challenged by chronic hunger, and an obvious need for the basic necessities of life... adequate shelter, food and clothing, it is incumbent upon all of us to heed the lesson Jesus taught in Matthew 25: 35-36, 40.

> *Come, you that are blessed by my Father, inherit the kingdom prepared for you from the foundation of the world; for I was hungry and you gave me food, I was thirsty and you gave me something to drink, I was a stranger and you welcomed me, I was naked and you gave me clothing, I was sick and you took care of me, I was in prison and you visited me.'*

> *... Truly I tell you, just as you did it to one of the least of these who are members of my family, you did it to me.* NRSV

Extending ourselves through volunteering and supporting charitable causes is mandatory for our own spiritual and personal growth. If you have ever seen one of the many television programs about hoarders, you will understand how holding onto everything leaves little or no space for spiritual expansion and true inner peace. Hanging onto emotional, and physical baggage eliminates the possibility for new people, experiences, and things to come forth. In other words, if we are not willing to release things and to share our gifts, we are in actuality blocking our blessings.

My point is if we don't obey the law of giving and receiving by sharing our gifts, whatever they may be, we will surely lose them just as easily as they come to us.

Do you support the source of your spiritual gifts?

Are you sharing your talents with your community?

How much time do you spend making life better for someone else?

> *Give, and you will receive. Your gift will return to you in full—pressed down, shaken together to make room for more, running over, and poured into your lap. The amount you give will determine the amount you get back.*
>
> *Luke 6:38*

Exercise 8

I encourage everyone to do the following – in no particular order:

- Identify your source of spiritual growth and establish a routine of making a contribution on a regular basis. Your contribution may be in the form of cash, material items or volunteering.
- Go through your home at least three to four times a year and gather up all the clothes and household items that you have not used in three years. Donate them to a local charity. I seek out homeless shelters, shelters for victims of domestic violence and centers that support young people who are leaving the foster care system.
- Spend time volunteering. There are all sorts of opportunities to volunteer in every community. Most communities have a volunteer clearinghouse where you can sign up to offer your services in any number of ways. These volunteer clearinghouses are often operated or funded by the United Way. I urge you to contact your local United Way office and inquire about the volunteer clearinghouse in your area.

AS YOU GIVE, SO SHALL YOU RECEIVE.

CHAPTER 9

Walk Fearlessly Through Life

There is no fear in love. But perfect love drives out fear, because fear has to do with punishment.

– 1 John 4:18

A Course in Miracles teaches that there are only two emotions – love and fear. We are all endowed with the gift of free will. Through that free will, we have a choice. We can choose to live in love or to live in fear.

Living in love leaves us open to receiving all the grace and blessings that await us from God... the source of all that is good. Living in fear can result in our refusal to accept those blessings. We must be willing to walk though life in confidence, knowing that God is with us always.

Common sense is a great gift from God that we must never ignore. Wisdom, discernment and faith are but three of the Twelve Powers identified by Unity co-founder Charles Fillmore as our most important gifts from God. This does not mean taking foolish chances or testing God's love and protection. If you are walking down a deserted, dimly street at 11:30 PM, do not turn into a dark alleyway to prove that God is with you.

We must at all times rest in the silence and take time to develop the ability to intuitively know when God is the source of an opportunity to fulfill a dream... to answer a prayer long held in our hearts. We develop this intuitive skill through affirmative prayer, claiming our highest good and the highest good for the world and through meditation, spending time in the silence, remaining open to that still small voice from deep within – the knowing that we are divinely guided at all times and in all things.

What have you been longing for?

What have you wanted to see manifested in your life that has alluded you?

What are your dreams?

Nobody can answer these questions for you. They don't lie hidden in any book or computer program. To enjoy the prosperity that God has given you, it is essential that you continue all the practices discussed in this little book.

- Create your own labels.
- Don't accept anyone else's definition of who you are or who you should be.
- Love yourself.
- Let go and let God.
- Forgive yourself and others.
- Back away from negative music, television shows and movies.
- Know that your good is already there – just waiting for you to claim it.
- Understand that there is no lack in the universe.
- Share your blessings and they will be multiplied accordingly.

As you walk fearlessly through life, always remember Shakespeare's quote in Hamlet "to thine own self be true." We will never be able to achieve spiritual prosperity or grow into the blessed happy beings God meant for us to be if we are not true to our own spirits.

Exercise 9

I conclude this book with the fifth Unity Principle: *"Knowing and understanding the laws of life, also called Truth, are not enough. A person must also live the Truth that he or she knows"*.

By living the truths we know to be ours, by diligently following the exercises at the end of each of these chapters and by claiming our truth… that we are indeed one with God and with the Universe, we are empowered to get rid of all the false beliefs we had about ourselves and move forward as the living, breathing Christ beings we truly are.

Namaste'.

BIBLIOGRAPHY

Scott, Jill and Bell, Anthony – *Golden* from *Beautiful Human: Words and Sounds Vol. 2*. Hidden Beach Recordings. 2004

The American Heritage Dictionary of the English Language. Houghton Mifflin Company. 2007

Addington, Jack and Cornelia - *All About Prosperity and How You Can Prosper.* DeVorss and Company. 1984

A Course in Miracles. Foundation for Inner Peace. 1996

Cosby, Bill - *I Started Out As A Child*. Warner Brothers Records. 1964

Shinn, Florence Scovel – *The Game of Life and How to Play It.* Simon and Schuster, Inc. 1986

www.dailyom.com

New Oxford Annotated Bible 3rd edition – New Revised Standard Version. 2001

Kahlil, Gibran – *The Prophet*. Alfred A. Knopf. 2004

Smith, Stretton – *Stretton Smith's 4T Prosperity Program*. The 4T Publishing Company. 1998

Ponder, Catherine – *The Prospering Power of Love*. DeVorss and Company. 1983

Byrne, Rhonda – *The Secret.* Atria Books. 2006

Dyer, Wayne – *Ten Secrets for Success and Inner Peace*. Hay House. 2002

Finley, Guy – *Weekly Key Lesson.* Life of Learning Foundation. www.guyfinley.org

Fillmore, Charles – *Prosperity.* Unity School of
Christianity. 1983

West, Georgia Tree – Prosperity's 10 Commandments.
Unity House. 1996

Babbs, John – *Divine Hotline: One Man's Journey Into
Creativity.* Cloud River Publishing Co.
1987

RECOMMENDED READING

(Some of these may be out of print. If that is the case, they should be available through on-line services and bookstores that specialize in used books.

Daily Word – bi-monthly magazine. Unity Books

Brumet, Robert – *The Quest for Wholeness*. Unity Books. 2002

Butterworth, Eric – *Discover The Power Within You*. Harper Collins Publishers. 1989

Casey, Karen – *Daily Meditations for Practicing The Course*. Harper Collins Publishers. 1995

DeBono, Edward – Handbook for the Positive Revolution. Viking Press. 1992

Hasbrouck, Hypatia – Handbook of Positive Prayer. Unity House. 2005

Fillmore, Lowell – The Prayer Way to Health, Wealth and Happiness. Unity Classic Library. 2000

Fillmore, Myrtle – How to Let God Help You. Unity Classic Library. 2007

Keys, Ken Jr., Penny, et al. – Gathering Power Through Insight and Love. Living Love Productions. 1987

Pagels, Elaine – *The Gnostic Gospels*. Vintage Books. 1989

Raphael Cushnir – *Setting Your Heart on Fire*. Broadway Books. 2003

Rosemergy, Jim – *Even Mystics Have Bills To Pay*. Unity House. 2000

Singh, Tara – Commentaries on A Course in Miracles. Harper Collins Publishers. 1992

Shinn, Frances Scovel – Your Word is Your Wand. DeVorss Publications.

Smoley, Richard – Forbidden Faith. Harper Collins Publishers. 2005

Tolle, Eckhart – *A New Earth: Awakening to Your Life's Purpose.* Namaste. 2005

Tolle, Eckhart – *The Power of Now.* Namaste. 2010

Witherspoon, Thomas E. – *Myrtle Fillmore Mother of Unity.* Unity Books. 2000

INTERNET RESOURCES

unity.org

dailyword.com

youtube.com: search for yellow brick cinema

acim.org

miraclecenter.org

pathwaysoflight.org

guyfinley.org

dailyom.com

ABOUT THE AUTHOR

Vernelle Nelson was introduced to Unity in the mid1980s. She is an ordained Unity minister who left the frigid winters, ice and snow in her hometown of Washington, DC for the sunshine and warm climate of South Florida in 1995.

She is the Founding Minister of Unity Golden Life Ministries, best known for Seaside Morning Meditation services near Ft. Lauderdale, Florida. Through Unity Golden Life Ministries, she also facilitates workshops, seminars and retreats at New Thought centers throughout the US. The most important work of Unity Golden Life Ministries, however, is providing pastoral care for the homebound, hospital visitations and spiritual support for hospice patients and their circle of care.

In 2016, Rev. Vernelle was honored to have been invited to contribute her insights in *A Sound of Unity: The Twelve Powers*, a movie about the Twelve Powers of man as taught by Unity co-founder, Charles Fillmore. This film is the brainchild of renowned New Thought author and director, James Twyman and was released in January 2017.

Reach out to Rev. Vernelle through Unity Golden Life Ministries:
754.252.5939
P.O. Box 26238　▪　Tamarac, FL 33320
unitygoldenlife@gmail.com
www.unitygoldenlife.org
www.facebook.com/UnityGoldenLifeMinistries

Made in the USA
Columbia, SC
20 February 2022

56235775R00049